HIPPOS

Published by Creative Education, Inc., 123 South Broad Street, Mankato, Minnesota
56001

Library of Congress Cataloging-in-Publication Data

Brust, Beth Wagner.
Hippos / by Beth Wagner Brust.
p.   cm. — (Zoobooks)
Summary: Describes the two different types of hippos, how they swim, what they eat,
and how they live in herds.
ISBN 0-88682-424-9
1. Hippopotamus—Juvenile literature. [1. Hippopotamus.] I. Title.
QL737.U57B78   1991   599.73'4—dc20   91-11643 CIP AC

HIPPOS

Series Created by
John Bonnett Wexo

Written by
Beth Wagner Brust

Zoological Consultant
Charles R. Schroeder, D.V.M.
Director Emeritus
San Diego Zoo &
San Diego Wild Animal Park

Scientific Consultant
Phil Robinson, D.V.M.
University of California
San Diego

International Union for the
Conservation of Nature
Hippo Specialst Group

Creative Education

Art Credits

Paintings by John Francis. **Activities Art** by Tran Lóc and John Francis.

Photographic Credits

Cover: Leonard Lee Rue III (Photo Researchers); **Pages Six and Seven**: N. Myers (Bruce Coleman, Inc.); **Page Eight:** Simon Trevor/ D.B. (Bruce Coleman, Inc.); **Page Nine:** Norman R. Lightfoot (Bruce Coleman, Ltd.); **Page Eleven:** Bruce Coleman (Bruce Coleman, Ltd.); **Page Thirteen: Top,** Animals Animals; **Bottom,** Edward R. Degginger (Bruce Coleman, Inc.); **Pages Fourteen and Fifteen:** © Frans Lanting; **Page Sixteen:** Henry Ausloos (Animals Animals); **Page Seventeen:** Top, Peter Davey (Bruce Coleman, Inc.); **Center,** Henry Ausloos (Animals Animals); **Bottom,** E.R. Degginger (Bruce Coleman, Inc.); **Page Nineteen: Top,** Marion H. Levy (Photo Researchers); **Bottom,** Len Rue Jr. (FPG International); **Pages Twenty and Twenty-one:** Charles Pierson (West Stock); **Page Twenty-two:** Leonard Lee Rue III (FPG International).

Our Thanks To: Michaele Robinson and Jerry Hurst, (San Diego Zoo Library); Carol Prime; Joe Selig; Paul Brust; Sean Brust.

Contents

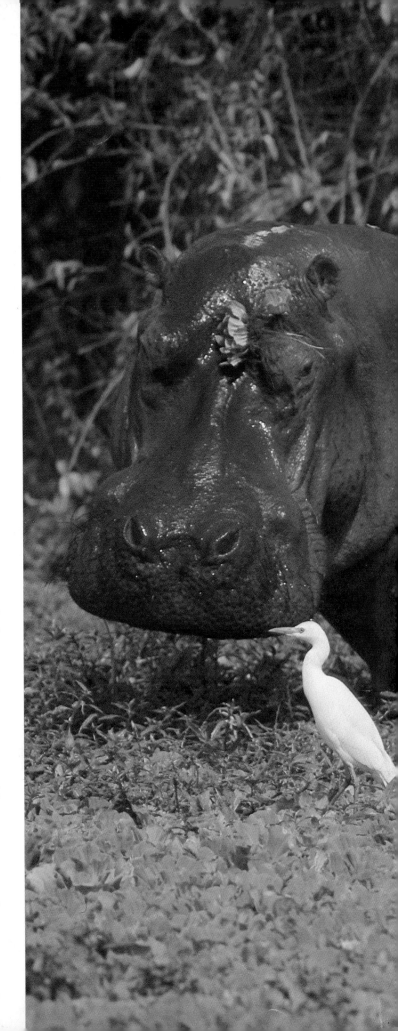

Hippopotamuses are, without a doubt, one of the strangest-looking animals in the world. But when they cuddle together in the muddy water, resting their huge heads on each other's backs, they are almost irresistible.

The ancient Greeks named these large, lumbering animals "hippopotamos," which means "river horse." But hippos are actually more closely related to pigs than to horses. Pigs and hippos both love mud. They have similar eyes, ears, and hoofs. And both have very round bodies.

Found only in Africa, hippos come in two varieties. The small *pygmy hippo* lives in rain forests and swamps. And the gigantic *common hippo* lives mostly in rivers and lakes.

The common hippo is the third largest land mammal in the world. It weighs almost as much as the White rhinoceros. But it weighs much less than the heaviest animal, the elephant. An African elephant at 12,000 pounds (5,500 kilograms) is twice as heavy as the common hippo.

The hippo is the only large land mammal that is *not* endangered. In preserves, hippos are even *increasing* in number. Why are common hippos doing so well? For one thing, they are not constantly hunted by humans. Many *have* been killed for meat or sport. But they are not wanted for their tusks. *And* they live a long time. In the wild, hippos live 20 to 40 years.

But there are two other important reasons why hippos survive so well. First, hippos don't have to run away when they sense trouble. They just hide underwater. Second, hippos are *nocturnal* (knock-TURN-ul). This means that they sleep during the day and feed at night. Feeding in the dark is much safer than feeding in daylight.

Hippos are awkward on land. But underwater, a magical change takes place. The hippo loses its clumsiness and glides through the water in a graceful, slow-motion ballet.

The only way to tell one hippo from another is by their scars, ear cuts, or deformed tails. During the day, males and females look alike because they are covered with mud or water. And at night, when they feed on land, it's too hard for scientists to study them. That's why there is still much to be learned about hippos.

Hippos get along well with birds like this egret. Birds help hippos stay healthy by eating the parasites that burrow in their hides.

It's easy to tell the two types of hippopotamuses apart—because they *look so different.*

Common hippos are much bigger than their cousins, the pygmy hippos. Common hippos can weigh 4,000 to 8,000 pounds (1,800 to 3,600 kilograms). Pygmy hippos weigh only 400 pounds (180 kilograms), or about as much as a large hog.

Common hippos are 13 to 15 feet long (4 to 4½ meters). And they stand 5 feet tall at the shoulder (150 centimeters). That's twice as tall as pygmy hippos and three times as long.

Finally, common hippos are as big around as they are long. They have short, heavy legs and a huge head held up by a thick neck. Pygmy hippos have smaller heads. They also have longer legs and necks in relation to their bodies.

Pygmy hippos are so secretive, not much is known about them in the wild. They hide in forests and swamps, tunneling through the thick bushes. Pygmies are rare—it seems there have never been very many of them.

AFRICA

☐ *Areas where hippos live today*

Thousands of years ago, hippos roamed through Europe, Asia, and Africa. But today, they are only in Africa. Pygmy hippos are found in the forests of West Africa. The huge common hippos live in East and Central Africa near lakes and rivers.

COMMON HIPPOPOTAMUS
Hippopotamus amphibius

Often mistaken for floating logs, common hippos look like the muddy water where they spend their days. Waterbirds sometimes perch on top of their heads while looking for insects.

Pygmy hippos only eat plants—leaves, roots, shoots, and fallen fruits. They have fewer teeth than the common hippo.

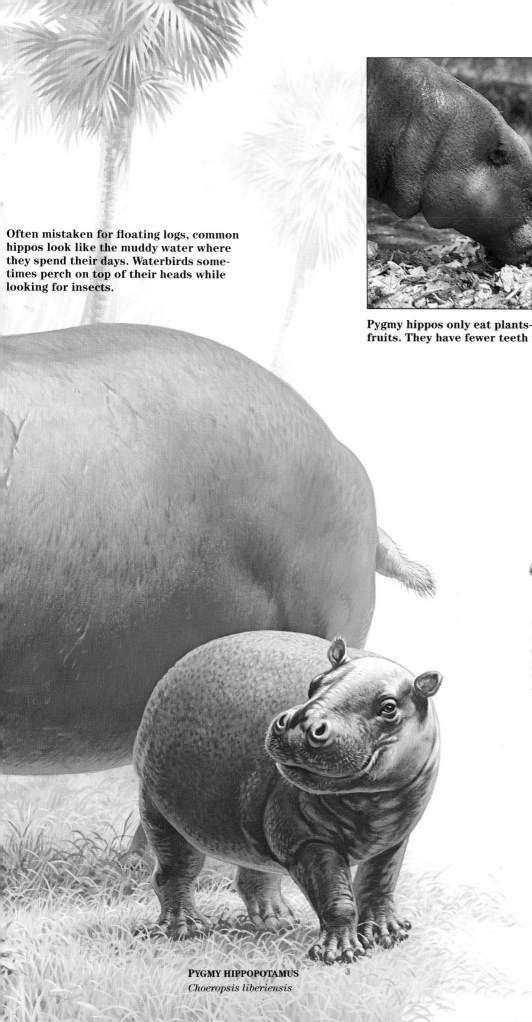

Common hippos spend most of their time in the water. So all four toes on each hoof are close together to help them swim more easily. Each toe works to support the hippo's tremendous weight out of water.

Pygmy hippos spend less time in the water than common hippos. Their toes are spread out to help them move more freely on land.

PYGMY HIPPOPOTAMUS
Choeropsis liberiensis

Water plays an important part in the lives of hippopotamuses. They hide in it. They sleep and rest in it during the daytime. And they use it to keep their skin moist. In the hot African sun, a hippo's skin can dry out very quickly. So to protect their skin, hippos either stay in the water or cover themselves with mud.

Hippos lead an *amphibious* (am-FIB-ee-us) life. They move from water to land—and then back to the water. They nap in shallow water or mudholes for most of the day. Then at dusk, they trudge inland to feed.

Hippos prefer slow-moving or still waters. When underwater, they can easily walk along the river bottom. Hippos cannot float, because their heavy muscles weigh them down—and cause them to sink. To stay on the water's surface, they have to paddle.

When diving, a hippo presses its ears flat against its head. This keeps most of the water out. When it surfaces, it shakes out the rest by wiggling its ears hard.

Before they dive, hippos take a deep breath and close their nostrils tightly. Adult hippos can stay underwater for as long as 5 or 6 minutes. When they come up, they exhale loudly, snorting and hissing as air blasts out of their nostrils.

Hippos are totally hairless except for some patches on the nose, ears, and tail. The hippo's tough hide oozes a sticky pink oil. This oil helps keep the animal's skin from drying out in the hot sun.

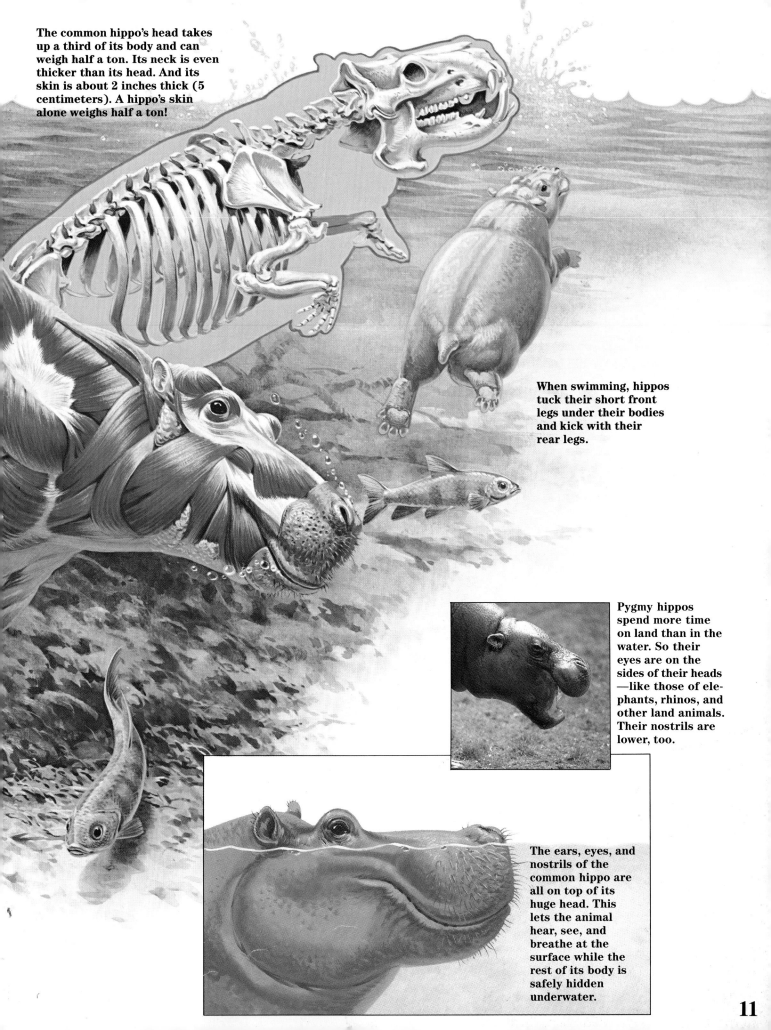

The common hippo's head takes up a third of its body and can weigh half a ton. Its neck is even thicker than its head. And its skin is about 2 inches thick (5 centimeters). A hippo's skin alone weighs half a ton!

When swimming, hippos tuck their short front legs under their bodies and kick with their rear legs.

Pygmy hippos spend more time on land than in the water. So their eyes are on the sides of their heads —like those of elephants, rhinos, and other land animals. Their nostrils are lower, too.

The ears, eyes, and nostrils of the common hippo are all on top of its huge head. This lets the animal hear, see, and breathe at the surface while the rest of its body is safely hidden underwater.

All hippos are plant-eating animals, or *herbivores* (URB-eh-voars). But even though hippos spend all day in the water, they rarely feed there. When it's time to eat, they head for the shore.

Every evening at sunset, these hungry giants waddle out of the water. They climb up steep banks and follow well-worn paths to graze in grassy fields. Then before sunrise, they follow the same paths back to their river, lake, or mudhole.

Hippos eat about 80 to 100 pounds (36 to 45 kilograms) of plants each night. And their favorite food is short grass. Hippos spend only about 5 or 6 hours a night grazing. Since the rest of their time is spent lying around in the water or mud, it's safe to say that eating is their main exercise.

For their size, hippos eat very little. Cows, for example, eat almost twice as much as hippos do. Scientists think that hippos eat less because they are experts at saving energy.

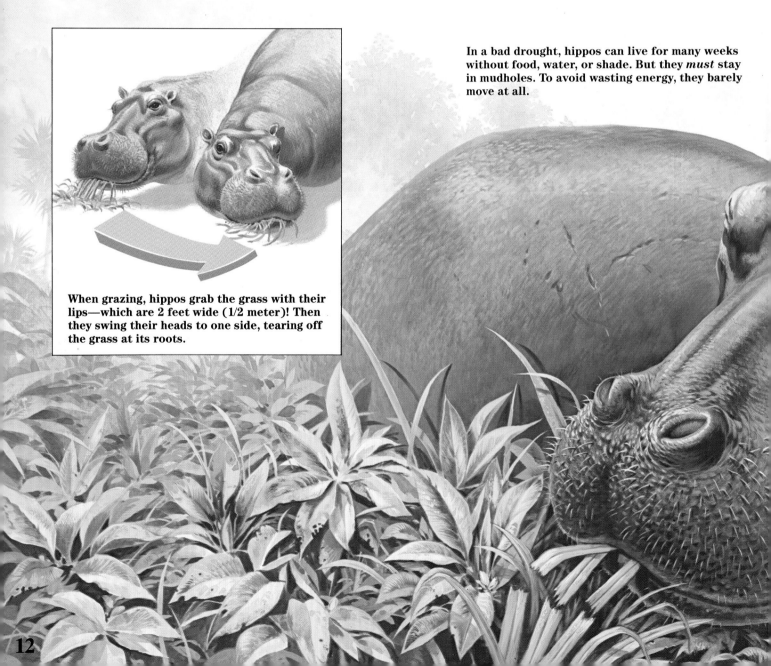

When grazing, hippos grab the grass with their lips—which are 2 feet wide (1/2 meter)! Then they swing their heads to one side, tearing off the grass at its roots.

In a bad drought, hippos can live for many weeks without food, water, or shade. But they *must* stay in mudholes. To avoid wasting energy, they barely move at all.

Hippos graze on the same land as buffaloes, elephants, antelopes, and warthogs. But because they eat mainly at night, they usually graze by themselves. Only at dusk are all the animals together.

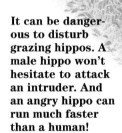

It can be dangerous to disturb grazing hippos. A male hippo won't hesitate to attack an intruder. And an angry hippo can run much faster than a human!

When grazing, hippos stay close to the water. The most they will ever walk to feed is about 6 miles (10 kilometers)—but usually they only go half that far.

*H*ippos are basically gentle animals. They would rather run away than fight. And because of their enormous size and sharp teeth, few animals try to attack them. Mostly hippos fight each other.

Male hippos fight over leadership of a herd. Or they fight over who has control of a water area or mudhole. When two hippos clash, it becomes a contest of weight and strength.

Most hippo fights take place in the water. The opponents move backwards side by side in a circle. Then, like two sledgehammers, they swing their massive heads toward each other and ram their open mouths together.

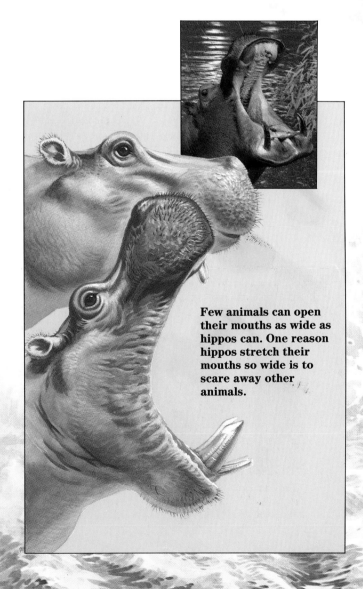

Few animals can open their mouths as wide as hippos can. One reason hippos stretch their mouths so wide is to scare away other animals.

When hippos fight, they use their razor-sharp teeth as weapons.

When fighting, hippos use their mouths like buckets to toss water at each other. They also grunt, growl, snort, bellow, and honk. With each charge, they make a ground-shaking, rumbling noise.

The common hippo has two tusk-like canine teeth in its lower jaw. Hippo canines can be up to *20 inches long* (50 centimeters), and can weigh *over 4 pounds* (2 kilograms) each. Like elephant tusks, a hippo's canines keep growing throughout the animal's life.

Hippos often fight for up to 2 hours, with only short rests. The longest hippo fight on record lasted 8 hours!

Young or old, almost all hippos are scarred from fighting. Their body organs and muscles are protected by a layer of fat under their thick hide.

A hippo mother and her young make up the basic hippo family. Hippos gather in herds of 15 to 30 members. But sometimes, as many as 150 hippos crowd together. A male always leads the herd's females and babies.

All hippo mothers protect their young. If anything or anyone gets between a mother and her babies, she gets fighting mad.

Mother hippos often form *nurseries*. They choose the flattest sandy beach near water. Then one or two mothers watch all the herd's babies—up to 40 young hippos. This frees the other mothers to swim and mate.

Young hippos are easy prey for lions, leopards, hyenas, and crocodiles. So mother hippos must always keep a sharp eye out for trouble. With their powerful jaws, mothers have been known to kill lions and bite crocodiles in half. Young hippos always hide behind their mother for protection.

Baby common hippos can swim before they can walk. It's a good thing, too, because sometimes they are born underwater and must come up for air right away. Babies can only hold their breath for 20 seconds.

Considering how enormous their parents are, baby common hippos are rather small. They only weigh 100 pounds (45 kilograms) at birth. An adult hippo can be 80 times bigger than a baby hippo!

A mother hippo looks after several babies at a time. And she is very strict about keeping them in a single-file line behind her. If any babies wander away or play in line, she nudges or nips at them to get back into position.

Hippos can do a very special trick. They can turn
each ear in a different direction at the same time.
As one ear turns forward, the other ear turns
backward.

N ow that you've read all about hippos, have some fun! The activities on these pages will let you see for yourself how much you've learned.

Hippo Word Puzzle

Complete each of the following sentences about hippos by listing the missing word on a piece of paper. (The number of boxes shows the number of letters in the missing word.) Then look at the first letter in each word you wrote to discover a secret word.

• Mother hippos often form ■■■■■■■■■ in which one or two mothers watch all the herd's babies.

• Waterbirds sometimes perch on top of the heads of hippos while looking for ■■■■■■■ to eat.

• Hippos eat about 80 to 100 pounds of plants each night, ■■■■■■■ in grassy fields for 5 or 6 hours.

• All hippos are ■■■■■■■■■■ ; their favorite food is short grass.

• The canine ■■■■■ of common hippos can be up to 20 inches long and can weigh up to 4 pounds each.

Answers
Teeth
Herbivores
Grazing
Insects
Nurseries

Q: How does a hippo cheer?

A: Hip-Hippo-Hooray!

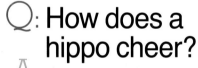

Can you unscramble these words?

Place where common hippos live:
W S P A S M

Where hippos like to hide:
D U W T E R N A E R

Where baby hippos are cared for:
U R S N E S I R E

Kind of teeth that common hippos have:
E N A C I N

What male hippos sometimes do:
I G F T H

Answers:
SWAMPS, UNDERWATER, NURSERIES, CANINE, FIGHT

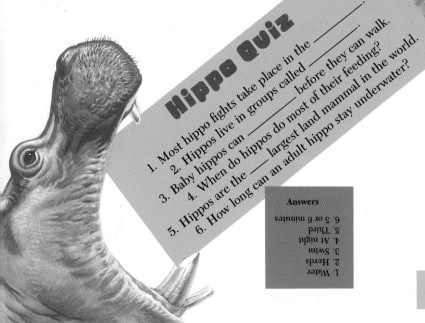

Hippo Quiz

1. Most hippo fights take place in the _____.
2. Hippos live in groups called _____.
3. Baby hippos can _____ before they can walk.
4. When do hippos do most of their feeding?
5. Hippos are the _____ largest land mammal in the world.
6. How long can an adult hippo stay underwater?

Answers
1. Water
2. Herds
3. Swim
4. At night
5. Third
6. 5 or 6 minutes

Make A Model Hippo

You'll need: clay, 2 beads or pebbles, toothpicks, an old toothbrush, and a scouring pad.

1 Think about the main shapes that make up the body of a hippo. Roll and model these shapes from clay.

2 Press the main shapes together. Pinch and smooth the clay to make the parts come together. Add more pieces of clay if you need to.

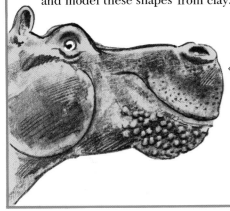

3 Form the ears and nostrils. Use beads or small pebbles for the eyes. Form a tail from the body. Shape the legs and feet.

4 Use a toothpick, old toothbrush, or scouring pad to add details and texture to your hippo. Now give your new friend a name.

How many hippopotamuses can you find in this picture?

Answer: 13

Index